The use of too m avoided, as it is m encourage comm to expect particula. ...

Care has been taken to retain sufficient realism in the illustrations and subject matter to enable a young child to have fun identifying objects, creatures and situations.

It is wise to remember that patience and understanding are very important, and that children do not all develop evenly or at the same rate. Parents should not be anxious if children do not give correct answers to those questions that are asked. With help, they will do so in their own time.

The brief notes at the back of this book will enable interested parents to make the fullest use of these **Ladybird talkabout** books.

Ladybird Books Loughborough

compiled by W. Murray

illustrated by Eric Winter and Harry Wingfield

The publishers wish to acknowledge the assistance of
the nursery school advisers who helped with the
preparation of this book,
especially that of Lady Britton, Chairman,
and Miss M Puddephat, M Ed, Vice Chairman
of The British Association for Early Childhood
Education (formerly The Nursery School Association).

talkabout
home

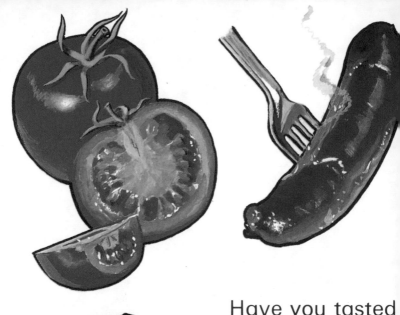

Have you tasted

any of these?

Have you seen

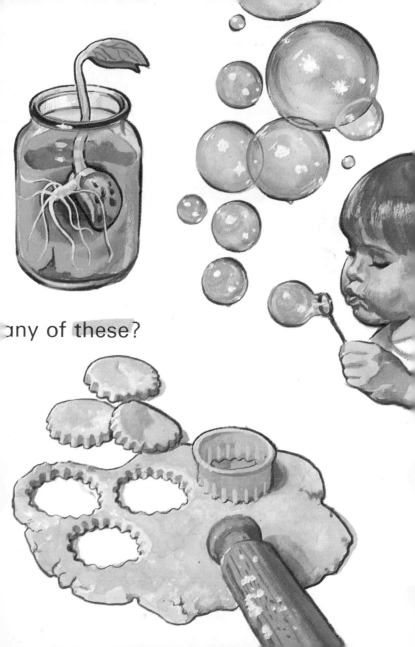

any of these?

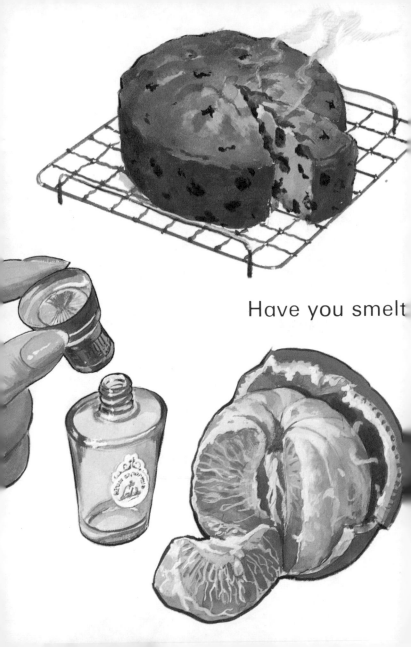

Have you smelt

any of these?

Have you heard

any of these?

Have you touched

any of these?

LOOK and find
another like this

and this

and this

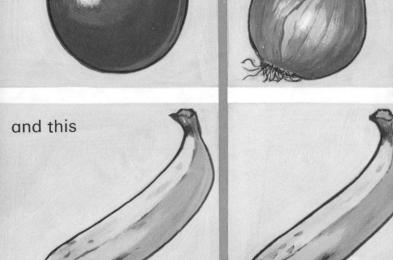

Talk about colours

Tell the story

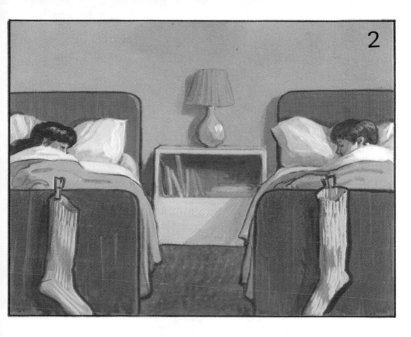

Which go together?

Counting fingers

1

2

3

4

5

Counting things

1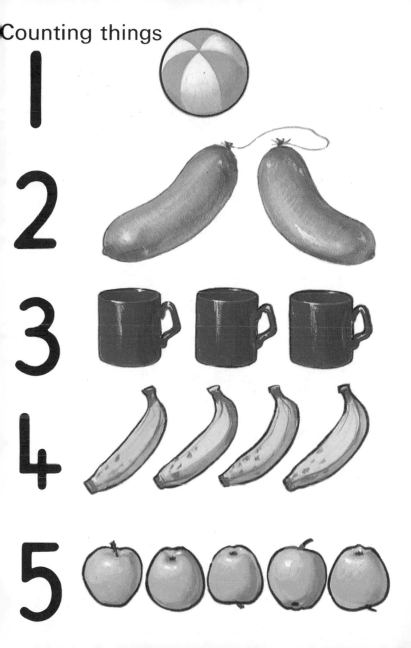

2

3

4

5

Talk about helping

Look for the sets

Tell the story

1

3

5

2

4

6

Talk about making music

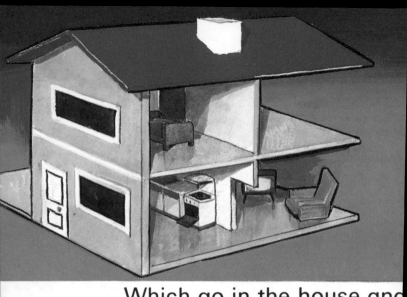

Which go in the house and

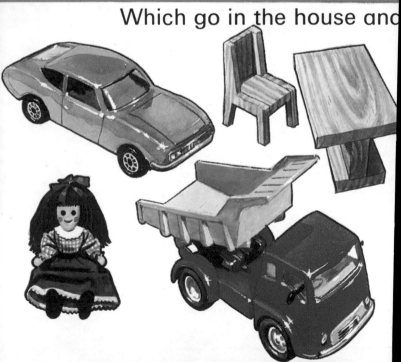

which go in the garage?

Talk about colours

Talk about the picture

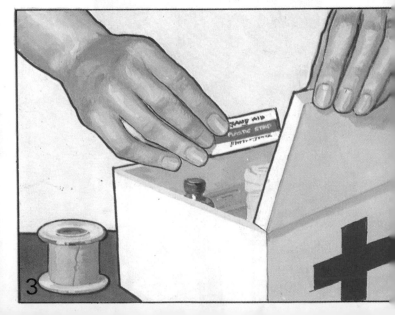

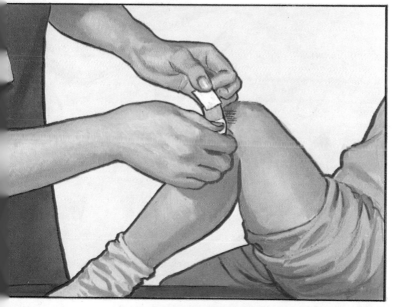

Whose ar

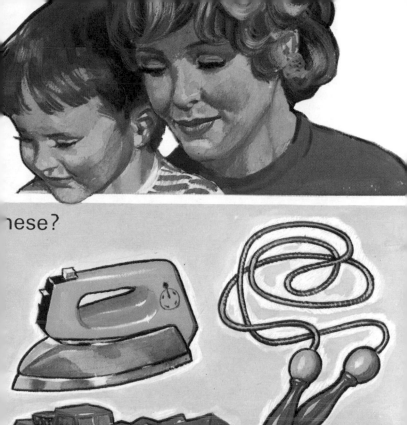

ese?

LOOK and find
another like this

and this

and this

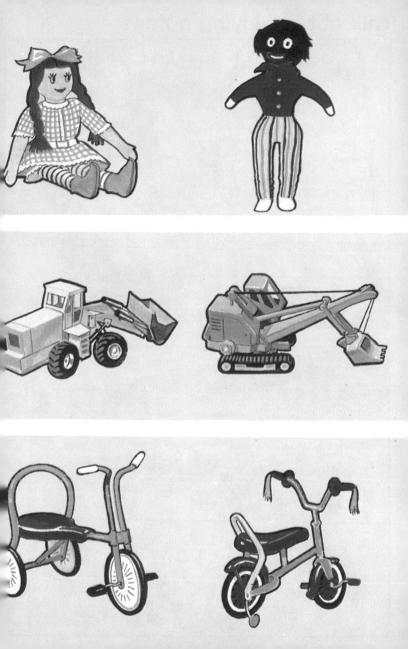

Talk about playing games

What are these for?

Suggestions for extending the use of this **talkabout** book . . .

The illustrations have been planned to help increase a child's vocabulary and under-standing, and the page headings are only brief suggestions as to how these illustrations can be used. For example, you could also talk about the sourness of the lemon pictured at the beginning of the book, about the banana being partly peeled and about the lemon, strawberries and tomato all having seeds – and so on.

In the rest of the book there are numerous opportunities for discussion on the use of the various articles shown, and where they may be found in the child's home. It could also be pointed out that one picture shows a hand **under** a tap, that the soap bubbles are going **up**, that the cat's fur is **soft**, the glass bottle **hard** and the ice **cold**, etc. These are concepts that a child needs to know and understand.

In many of the illustrations (for example, on the 'Look and find another like this' pages)